M IS FOR MATH

Dedicated to the memory of my dad who fostered my love of math - K.K.L.

For River, my little math lover - L.S.

Published in 2023 by 619 Wreath Publishing and Consulting

www.619Wreath.com

All rights reserved.

This book or any portion thereof may not be reproduced or used in any manner whatsoever without the express written permission of the publisher except for the use of brief quotations in a book review.

Text © 2023 Krystina K. Leganza | Illustrations © 2023 Lauren Staser

Illustrations were created digitally

Set in Garamond Premier

Designed by Lauren Staser

Print ISBN: 978-1-958469-12-5

M IS FOR MATH

written by:
KRYSTINA K. LEGANZA

illustrated by:
LAUREN STASER

The anteater added with the aid of an **abacus**.

The bear bought one **billion** blocks.

The chicken calculated the **circumference** of the **circle**.

The duck danced along the **diameter** of the **disc**.

The elephant eyed the **equals sign** in the **equation**.

The frog found **fractions** fascinating.

The giraffe gauged his growth on a **graph**.

The hare hopped happily along the **hypotenuse**.

The iguana insisted there is an **infinite** number of **integers**.

The jackrabbit joined the others in admiring the **Julia set**.

The kangaroo kept his ketchup in a **Klein bottle**.

The lion learned that **lines** are limitless.

The monkey measured the **Mobius band**.

The newt noticed the **numerator** was a **negative number**.

The octopus outlined **one octagon**.

The pig paced the **perimeter** of her pen.

The quail quivered under a quilt of **quadrilaterals**.

The rooster realized a **rectangle** has four **right angles**.

The spider spun a **square** web inside a **sphere**.

The turtles tiled the floor with **20 triangles**.

The urchin unveiled the **union** to the viper using a **Venn diagram**.

The worm wrote the **whole numbers** in his workbook.

The ox and the yak yelled across the **xy-plane**.

The zebra zigzagged through many **zeroes**.

Notes to Parents and Teachers

A few of my earliest memories are doing math problems with my dad as a preschooler. He made math so much fun. I want all children from a young age to realize and appreciate that math is fun and that there is so much more to math than numbers.

Several of the math terms in the book may be unfamiliar to some people. Below I have included simple explanations for each math term.

Abacus – an abacus is an instrument for performing calculations by sliding counters along vertical or horizontal rods

Billion – one billion is the number 1,000,000,000

Circumference – the circumference of a circle is the distance around the perimeter of the circle

Diameter – the diameter of a circle is a line segment between two points on the circle that goes through the center of the circle

Disc – a disc is either the interior of a circle or the interior of a circle and the circle itself

Equals Sign – the equals sign, denoted by the symbol "=", is used to indicate that two quantities or expressions are the same

Equation – an equation is a mathematical statement with an equals sign

Fraction – a fraction represents a part of a whole; it is a number which can be written as one number above a line (representing division) and another number below the line

Graph – a graph is a picture or drawing representing a relationship between quantities; there are many types of graphs: line, bar, pie, etc.

Hypotenuse – the hypotenuse is the longest side of a right triangle; it is opposite the right (90-degree) angle

Infinite – infinite is the idea that something has no end or bound; it cannot be measured

Integer – an integer is a number that is a whole number or the negative of a whole number; the set of integers consists of the numbers . . . -2, -1, 0, 1, 2, . . .

Julia Set – the Julia set is a special fractal; a fractal is a never-ending pattern that repeats itself in different scales; one can zoom in and see the same shape forever

Klein Bottle – a Klein bottle is a surface whose neck disappears into itself so that there is no inside or outside; a Klein bottle can only be constructed in four dimensions

Line – a line is a straight set of points that extend in opposite directions and continue forever

Mobius band – a Mobius band is loop with a twist; it has only one side

Numerator – the numerator is the top number of a fraction

Negative number – a negative number is a number less than zero

One – one is the number representing a single object

Octagon – an octagon is a polygon, a two-dimensional geometric figure, with eight sides

Perimeter – the perimeter is a closed path that surrounds a shape; it is also the distance around a shape

Quadrilateral – a quadrilateral is a polygon, a two-dimensional geometric figure, with four sides

Rectangle – a rectangle is a quadrilateral with two pairs of equal parallel sides and four right angles

Right angle – a right angle is a 90-degree angle

Square – a square is a rectangle with four equal sides

Sphere – a sphere is a three-dimensional object that is round

Triangle – a triangle is a polygon, a two-dimensional geometric figure, with three sides

Union – the union of sets is the set containing all of the objects from the given sets

Venn diagram – a Venn diagram is a picture representing the relationship between sets

Whole number – the whole numbers are the integers from zero to infinity: 0, 1, 2, 3, 4, 5, 6, . . .

xy-plane – the xy-plane, also known as the Cartesian plane, has two perpendicular axes, the x-axis and the y-axis

Zero – the number zero, denoted by the symbol "0", represents none

Acknowledgements

I want to thank Candice Price and Miloš Savić, 619 Wreath Publishing, for believing in my vision, offering great advice, and bringing this book to reality.

I also want to thank Lauren Staser for making the words and sentences come to life through her delightful illustrations.

Last but by no means least I want to thank my family and friends for their love and support.

KRYSTINA K. LEGANZA

May 2023

Printed in the USA
CPSIA information can be obtained
at www.ICGtesting.com
LVHW070235020823
754144LV00002B/19